Life
on the
Hard Shoulder

by the same author

BRILLIANT ADVICE!
MORE BRILLIANT ADVICE!

Life on the Hard Shoulder

by Annie Lawson

A Deirdre McDonald Book
BELLEW PUBLISHING
London

First published in 1990
by Deirdre McDonald Books
Bellew Publishing Co. Ltd.
7 Southampton Place, London WC1A 2DR

Copyright © Annie Lawson 1990

ISBN 0 947792 50 3

Printed in Hong Kong by
Regent Publishing Services Ltd

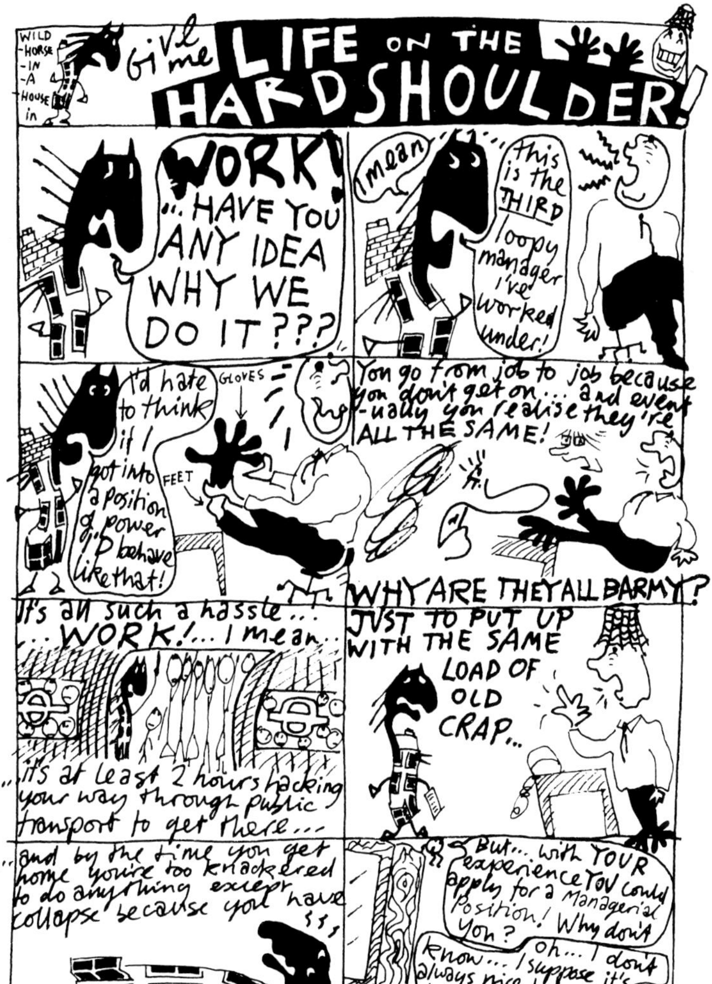

WILD -HORSE -IN -A HOUSE in
Givi me LIFE ON THE HARD SHOULDER!
WORK! ... HAVE YOU ANY IDEA WHY WE DO IT???
I mean
this is the THIRD loopy manager I've worked under!
I'd hate to think if I got into a position of power I'd behave like that!
GLOVES
FEET
You go from job to job because you don't get on... and event-ually you realise they're ALL THE SAME!
WHY ARE THEY ALL BARMY?
It's all such a hassle... ...WORK!... I mean...
...it's at least 2 hours hacking your way through public transport to get there...
JUST TO PUT UP WITH THE SAME LOAD OF OLD CRAP...
...and by the time you get home you're too knackered to do anything except collapse because you have
to get up & do the same load of old rubbish the next day!
But... with YOUR experience YOU could apply for a Managerial Position! Why don't you?
Oh... I don't know... I suppose it's always nice to be able to pass the buck...

WET LETTUCE, Pea and MANGO

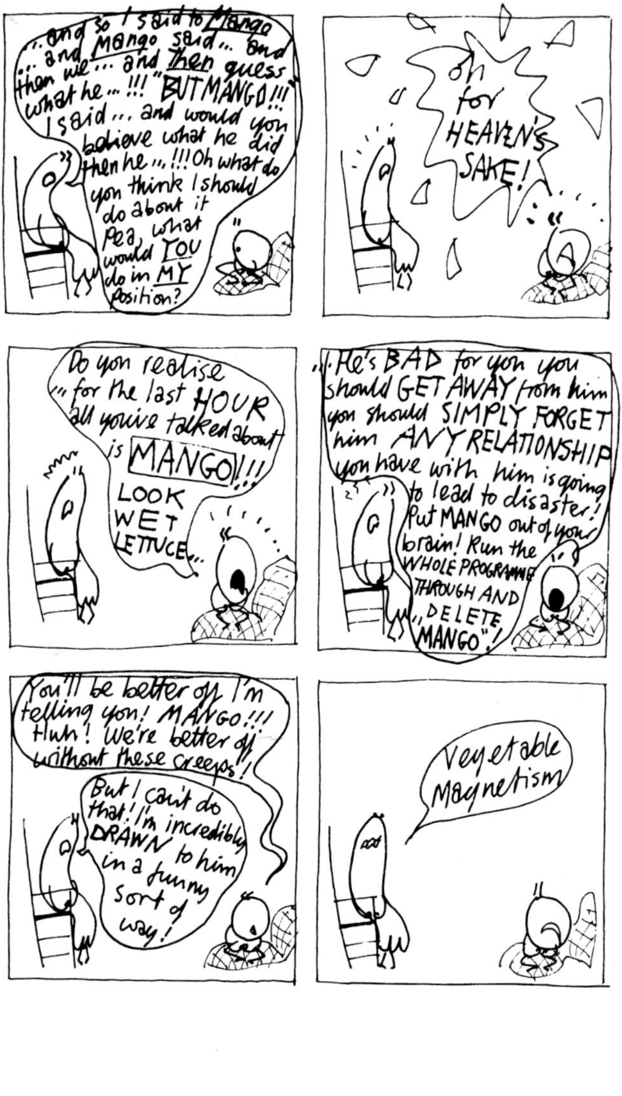
..and so I said to Mango ... and Mango said.. and then we ... and then guess what he ... !!! "BUT MANGO!!!" I said ... and would you believe what he did then he ...!!! Oh what do you think I should do about it Pea, what would YOU do in MY position?
oh for HEAVEN'S SAKE!
Do you realise ... for the last HOUR all you've talked about is MANGO!!! LOOK WET LETTUCE...
..He's BAD for you you should GET AWAY from him you should SIMPLY FORGET him ANY RELATIONSHIP you have with him is going to lead to disaster! Put MANGO out of your brain! Run the WHOLE PROGRAMME THROUGH AND "DELETE MANGO"!
You'll be better off I'm telling you! MANGO!!! Huh! We're better off without these creeps!
But I can't do that! I'm incredibly DRAWN to him in a funny sort of way!
Vegetable Magnetism

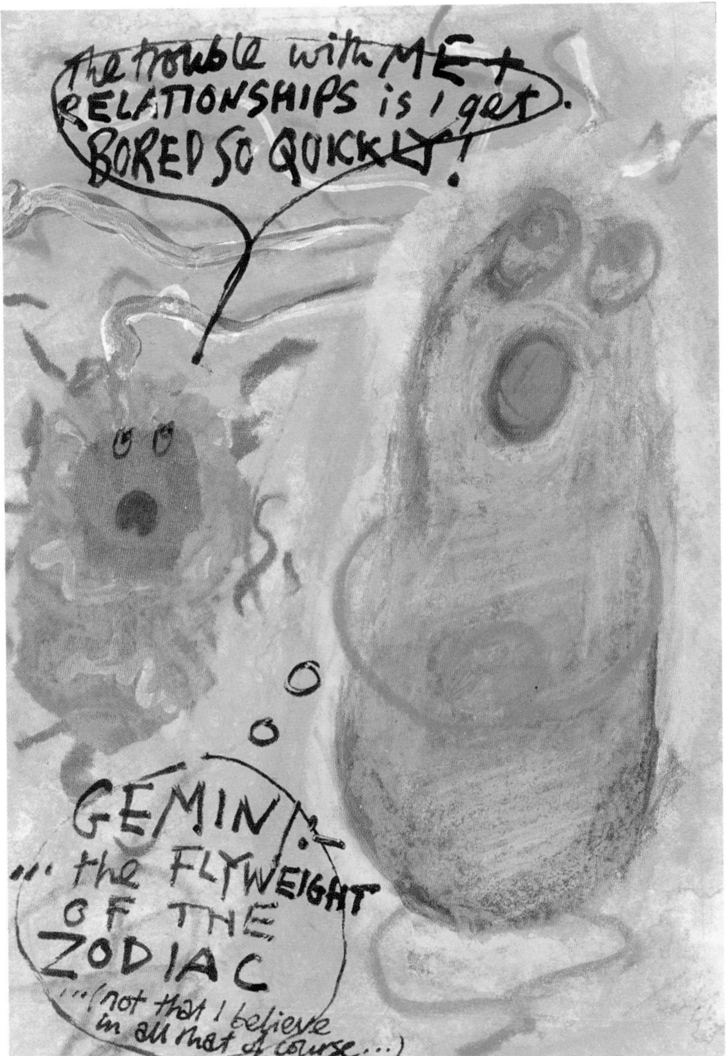
The trouble with ME + RELATIONSHIPS is I get BORED SO QUICKLY!
GEMINI:- ... the FLYWEIGHT OF THE ZODIAC
...(not that I believe in all that of course...)

I MEAN... ARE WOMEN MORE COMPLETE BEINGS?
I'm going out with this bloke right.. well .. what I mean is.. I frequent the pub where he hangs out with his mates...
...and if I'm lucky at 11.30 pm we go back to his place...
...whereas if I'm unlucky I have to wait around until 3am when after-hours drinking finishes
You should see this bloke's place!
How can he live in it??? The sink's always full of teabags... the milk's always festering...
...and I don't think he's ever heard of the invention of the bog roll!
Can you imagine putting your CAP in in a coal cellar with no light? conditions in the 3rd World must be better than this!

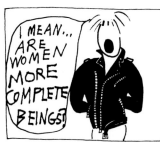

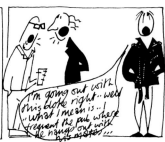

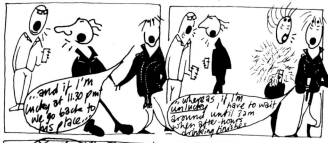

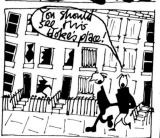

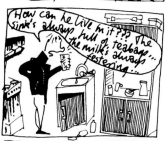

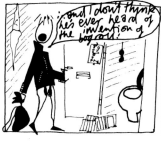

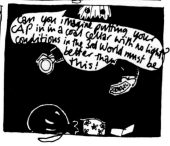

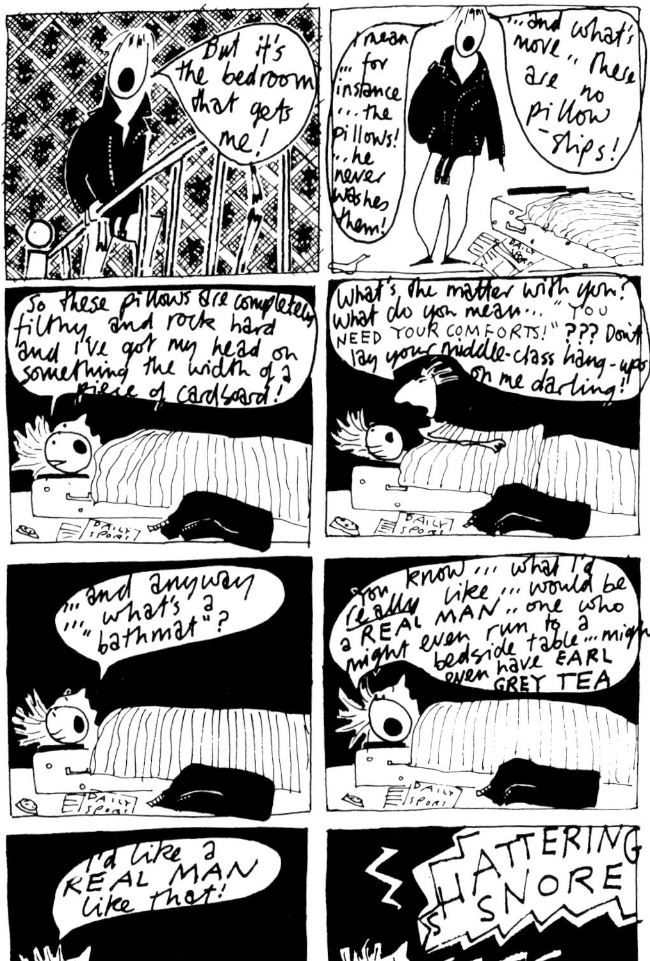
But it's the bedroom that gets me!
I mean ... for instance ... the pillows! .. he never washes them!
... and what's more .. there are no pillow -slips!
So these pillows are completely filthy and rock hard and I've got my head on something the width of a piece of cardboard!
What's the matter with you? What do you mean... "YOU NEED YOUR COMFORTS!" ??? Don't lay your middle-class hang-ups on me darling!
... and anyway ... what's a ... "bathmat"?
You know ... what I'd really like ... would be a REAL MAN .. one who might even run to a bedside table ... might even have EARL GREY TEA
I'd like a REAL MAN like that!
SHATTERING SNORE

WETLETTUCE Still can't stop

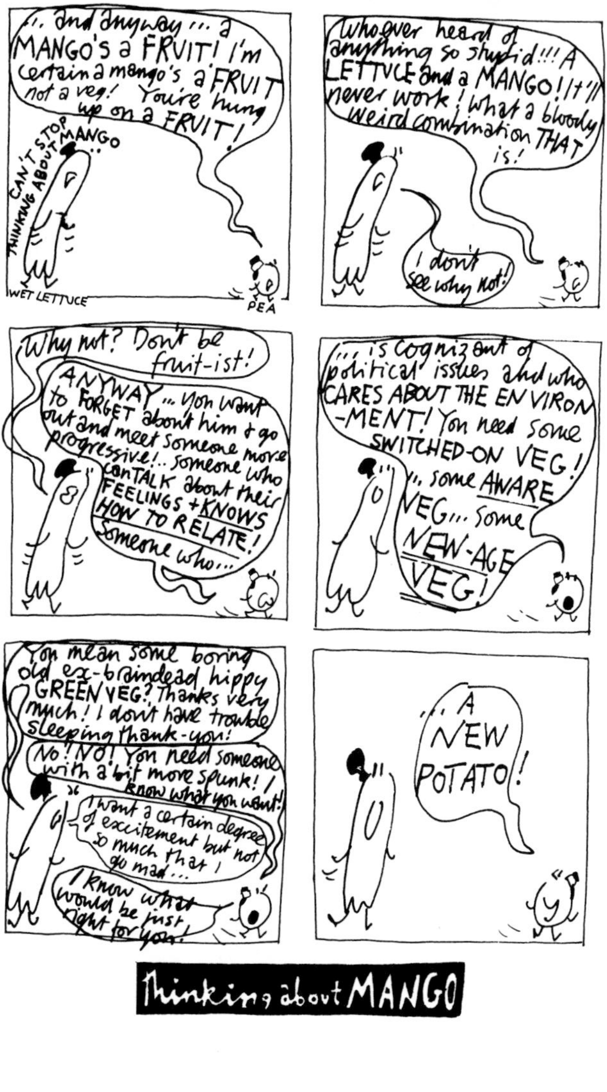

... and anyway ... a MANGO's a FRUIT! I'm certain a mango's a FRUIT not a veg! You're hung up on a FRUIT!
CAN'T STOP THINKING ABOUT MANGO
WET LETTUCE
PEA
Whoever heard of anything so stupid!!! A LETTUCE and a MANGO! It'll never work! What a bloody weird combination THAT is!
I don't see why not!
Why not? Don't be fruit-ist!
ANYWAY ... You want to FORGET about him & go out and meet someone more progressive! .. someone who can TALK about their FEELINGS + KNOWS HOW TO RELATE! Someone who...
... is cognizant of political issues and who CARES ABOUT THE ENVIRON-MENT! You need some SWITCHED-ON VEG! .. some AWARE VEG... some NEW-AGE VEG!
You mean some boring old ex-braindead hippy GREEN VEG? Thanks very much! I don't have trouble sleeping thank-you!
No! NO! You need someone with a bit more spunk! I know what you want!
I want a certain degree of excitement but not so much that I go mad...
I know what would be just right for you!
... A NEW POTATO!

Thinking about MANGO

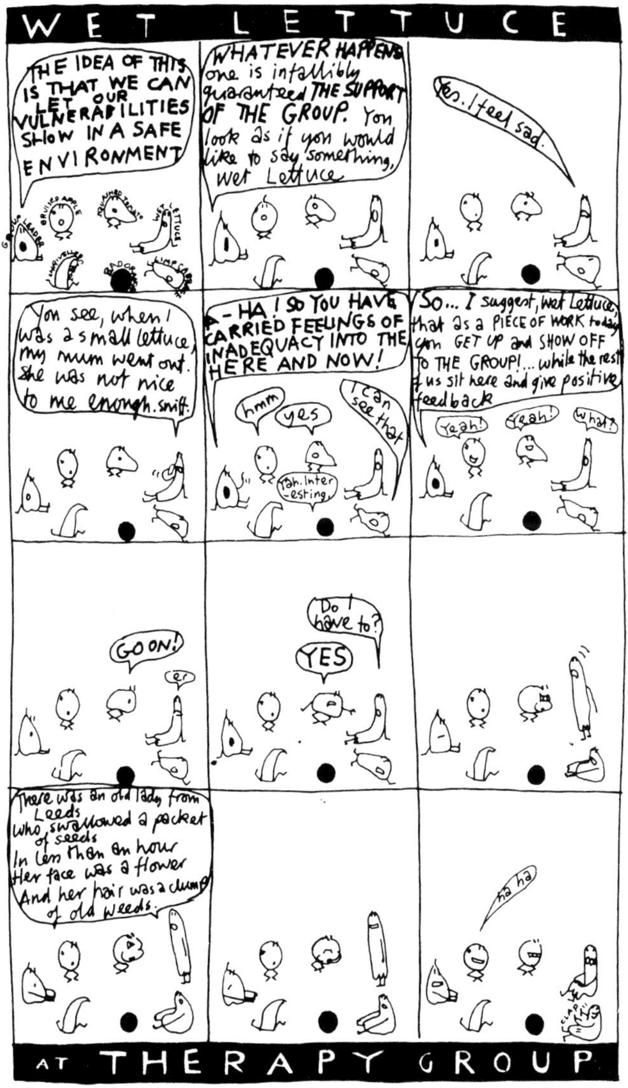
WET LETTUCE
THE IDEA OF THIS IS THAT WE CAN LET OUR VULNERABILITIES SHOW IN A SAFE ENVIRONMENT
GROUP LEADER
BRUISED APPLE
SQUASHED TOMATO
WET LETTUCE
WHATEVER HAPPENS one is infallibly guaranteed THE SUPPORT OF THE GROUP. You look as if you would like to say something, Wet Lettuce
Yes. I feel sad.
You see, when I was a small lettuce, my mum went out. She was not nice to me enough. sniff.
A-HA! SO YOU HAVE CARRIED FEELINGS OF INADEQUACY INTO THE HERE AND NOW!
hmm
yes
I can see that
Yah. Inter-esting.
So... I suggest, Wet Lettuce, that as a PIECE OF WORK today you GET UP and SHOW OFF TO THE GROUP!... while the rest of us sit here and give positive feedback
Yeah!
Yeah!
What?
GO ON!
er
Do I have to?
YES
There was an old lady from Leeds
Who swallowed a packet of seeds
In less than an hour
Her face was a flower
And her hair was a clump of old weeds.
ha ha
CLAP
AT THERAPY GROUP

The Gas Bill

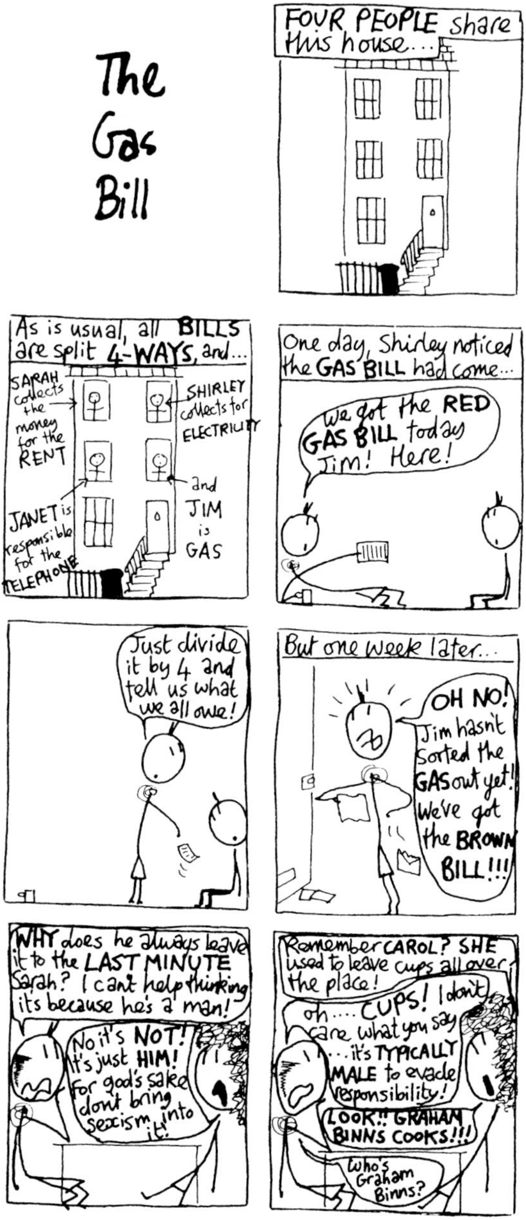
FOUR PEOPLE share this house...
As is usual, all BILLS are split 4-WAYS, and...
SARAH collects the money for the RENT
SHIRLEY collects for ELECTRICITY
JANET is responsible for the TELEPHONE
and JIM is GAS
One day, Shirley noticed the GAS BILL had come...
We got the RED GAS BILL today Jim! Here!
Just divide it by 4 and tell us what we all owe!
But one week later...
OH NO! Jim hasn't sorted the GAS out yet! We've got the BROWN BILL!!!
WHY does he always leave it to the LAST MINUTE Sarah? I can't help thinking its because he's a man!
No it's NOT! It's just HIM! For god's sake dont bring sexism into it!
Remember CAROL? SHE used to leave cups all over the place!
oh.... CUPS! I don't care what you say ...it's TYPICALLY MALE to evade responsibility!
LOOK!! GRAHAM BINNS COOKS!!!
Who's Graham Binns?

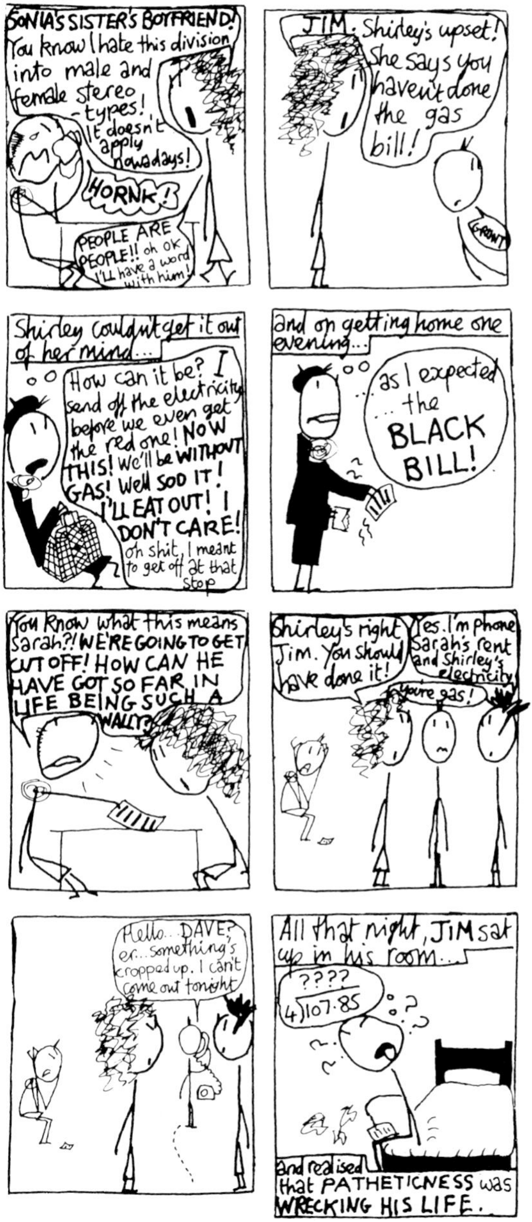
SONIA'S SISTER'S BOYFRIEND! You know I hate this division into male and female stereo-types! It doesn't apply nowadays!
HORNK!
PEOPLE ARE PEOPLE!! oh OK I'll have a word with him!
JIM, Shirley's upset! She says you haven't done the gas bill!
GROWT
Shirley couldn't get it out of her mind...
How can it be? I send off the electricity before we even get the red one! NOW THIS! We'll be WITHOUT GAS! Well SOD IT! I'LL EAT OUT! I DON'T CARE!
oh shit, I meant to get off at that stop
and on getting home one evening...
as I expected... the BLACK BILL!
You know what this means Sarah?! WE'RE GOING TO GET CUT OFF! HOW CAN HE HAVE GOT SO FAR IN LIFE BEING SUCH A WALLY?!
Shirley's right Jim. You should have done it!
Yes. I'm phone Sarah's rent and Shirley's electricity
You're gas!
Hello... DAVE? er... something's cropped up. I can't come out tonight
All that night, JIM sat up in his room...
????
4)107.85
and realised that PATHETICNESS was WRECKING HIS LIFE.

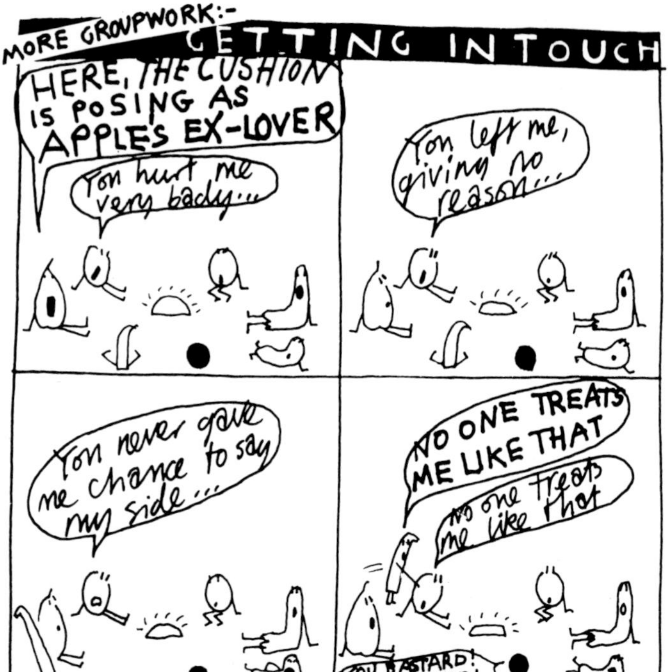
MORE GROUPWORK:- GETTING IN TOUCH
HERE, THE CUSHION IS POSING AS APPLE'S EX-LOVER
You hurt me very badly...
You left me, giving no reason...
You never gave me chance to say my side...
NO ONE TREATS ME LIKE THAT
No one treats me like that
YOU BASTARD! YOU BASTARD!
ARGH! HE REJECTED YOU! WASTE HIM!
STAMP ON HIM!
DO HIM IN! GO ON!
GET YOUR OWN BACK!
EXTERMINATE! EXTERMINATE!
KILL! KILL!
You bastard
STOP! I THINK HERE YOU'RE TALKING TO YOUR MOTHER
WITH ANGER

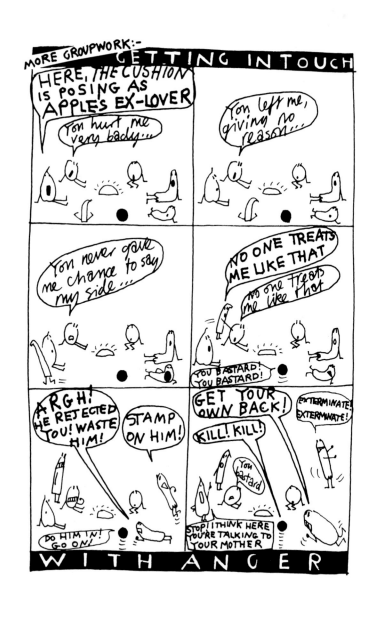

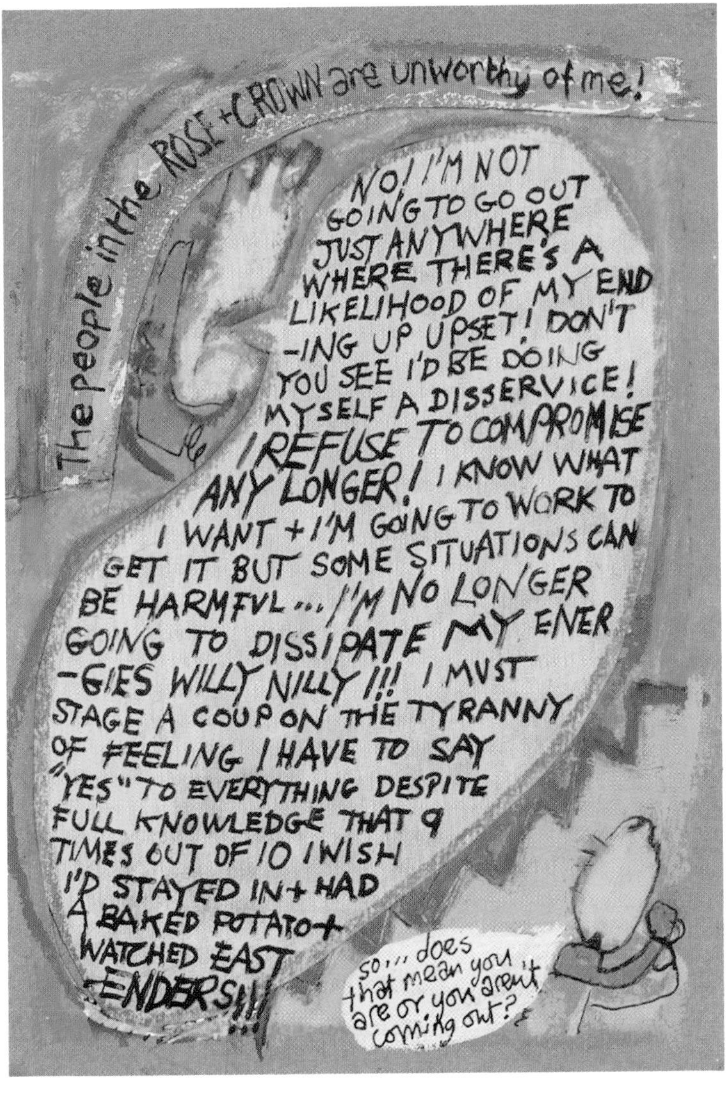
The people in the ROSE + CROWN are unworthy of me!
NO! I'M NOT GOING TO GO OUT JUST ANYWHERE WHERE THERE'S A LIKELIHOOD OF MY END-ING UP UPSET! DON'T YOU SEE I'D BE DOING MYSELF A DISSERVICE! I REFUSE TO COMPROMISE ANY LONGER! I KNOW WHAT I WANT + I'M GOING TO WORK TO GET IT BUT SOME SITUATIONS CAN BE HARMFUL... I'M NO LONGER GOING TO DISSIPATE MY ENER-GIES WILLY NILLY!!! I MUST STAGE A COUP ON THE TYRANNY OF FEELING I HAVE TO SAY "YES" TO EVERYTHING DESPITE FULL KNOWLEDGE THAT 9 TIMES OUT OF 10 I WISH I'D STAYED IN + HAD A BAKED POTATO + WATCHED EAST-ENDERS!!!
so... does that mean you are or you aren't coming out?

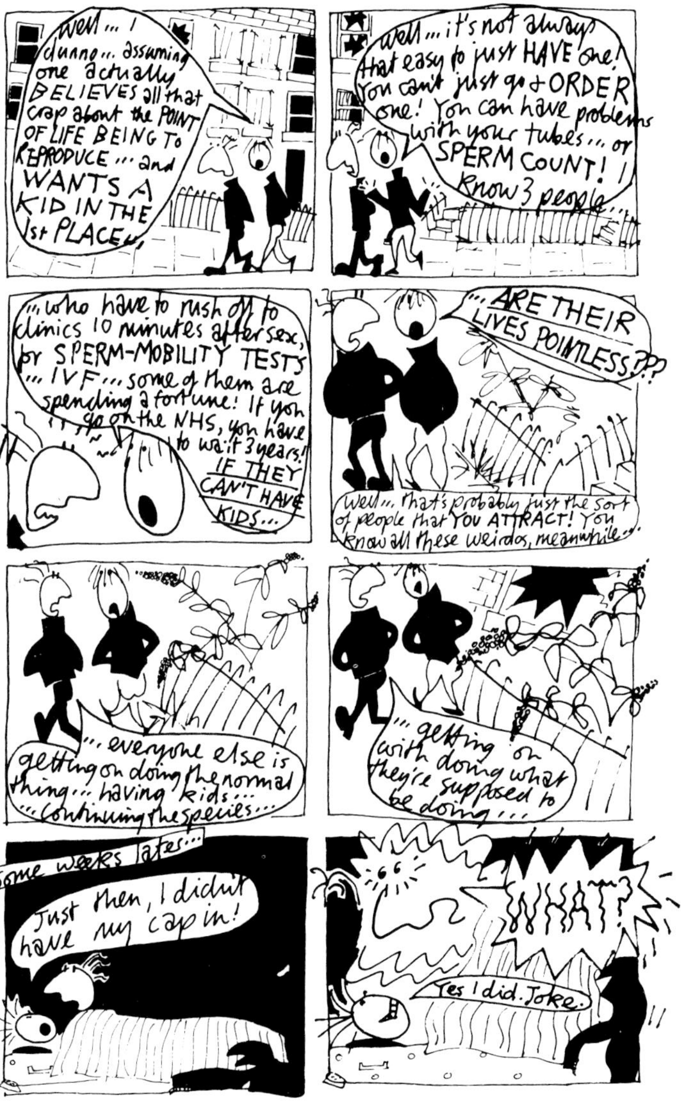
Well... I dunno... assuming one actually BELIEVES all that crap about the POINT OF LIFE BEING TO REPRODUCE... and WANTS A KID IN THE 1st PLACE...,
Well... it's not always that easy to just HAVE one! You can't just go + ORDER one! You can have problems with your tubes... or SPERM COUNT! I know 3 people...
...who have to rush off to clinics 10 minutes after sex, for SPERM-MOBILITY TESTS ... IVF... some of them are spending a fortune! If you go on the NHS, you have to wait 3 years! IF THEY CAN'T HAVE KIDS...
...ARE THEIR LIVES POINTLESS???
Well... that's probably just the sort of people that YOU ATTRACT! You know all these weirdos, meanwhile...
...everyone else is getting on doing the normal thing... having kids... ...continuing the species...
...getting on with doing what they're supposed to be doing...
Some weeks later...
Just then, I didn't have my cap in!
WHAT?
Yes I did. Joke.

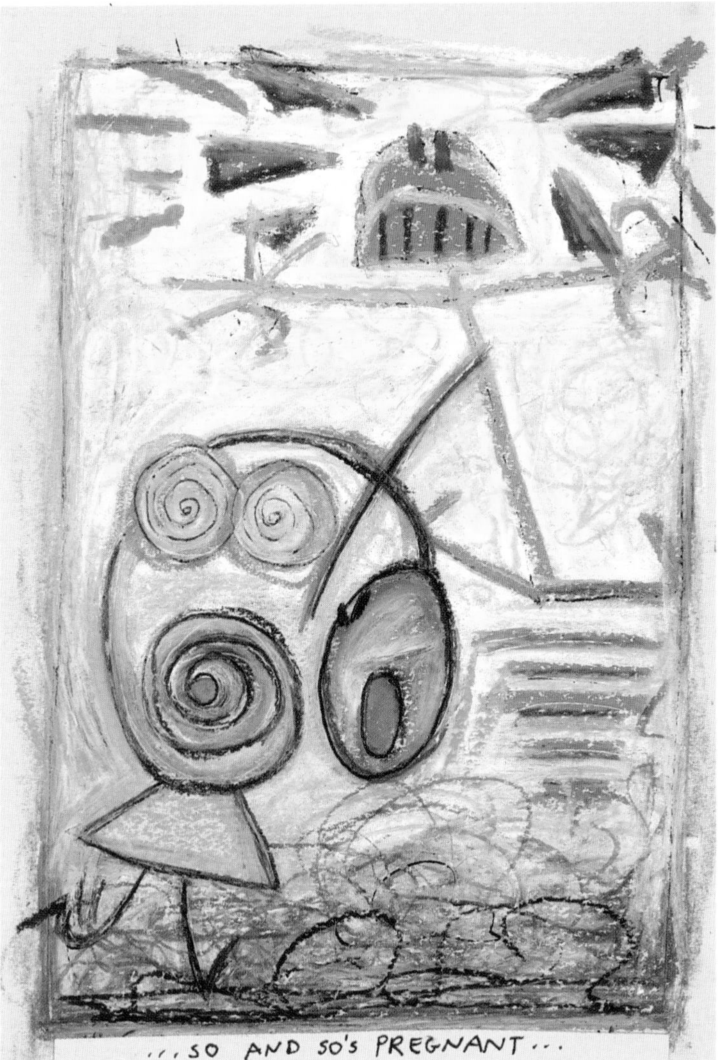
...SO AND SO'S PREGNANT...

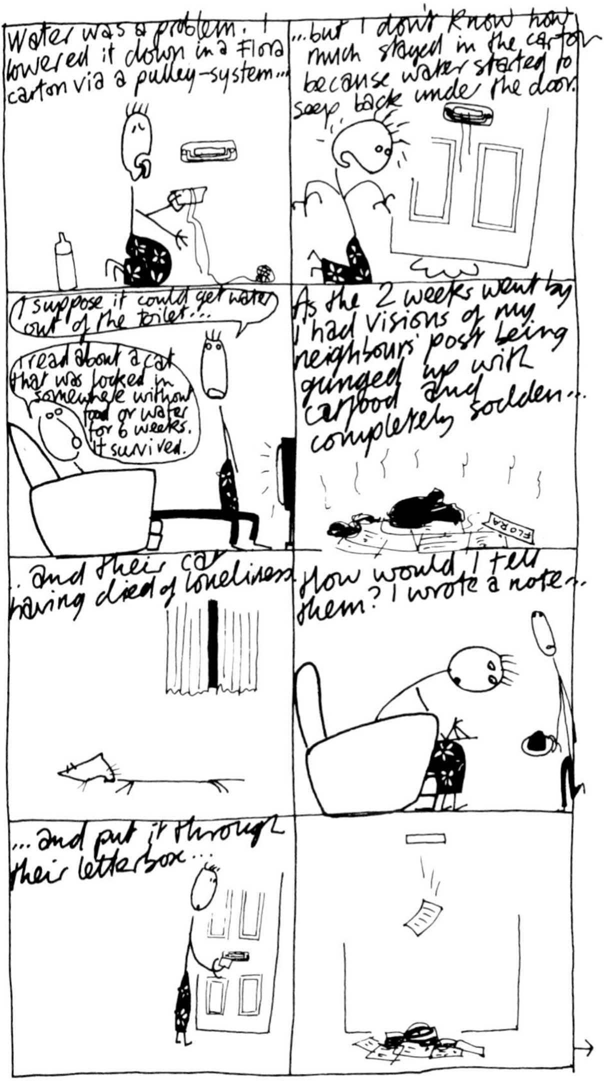
Water was a problem. I lowered it down in a Flora carton via a pulley-system...
...but I don't know how much stayed in the carton because water started to seep back unde the door.
I suppose it could get water out of the toilet...
I read about a cat that was locked in somewhere without food or water for 6 weeks. It survived.
As the 2 weeks went by I had visions of my neighbours' post being gunged up with catfood and completely sodden...
FLORA
...and their cat having died of loneliness.
How would I tell them? I wrote a note...
...and put it through their letterbox...

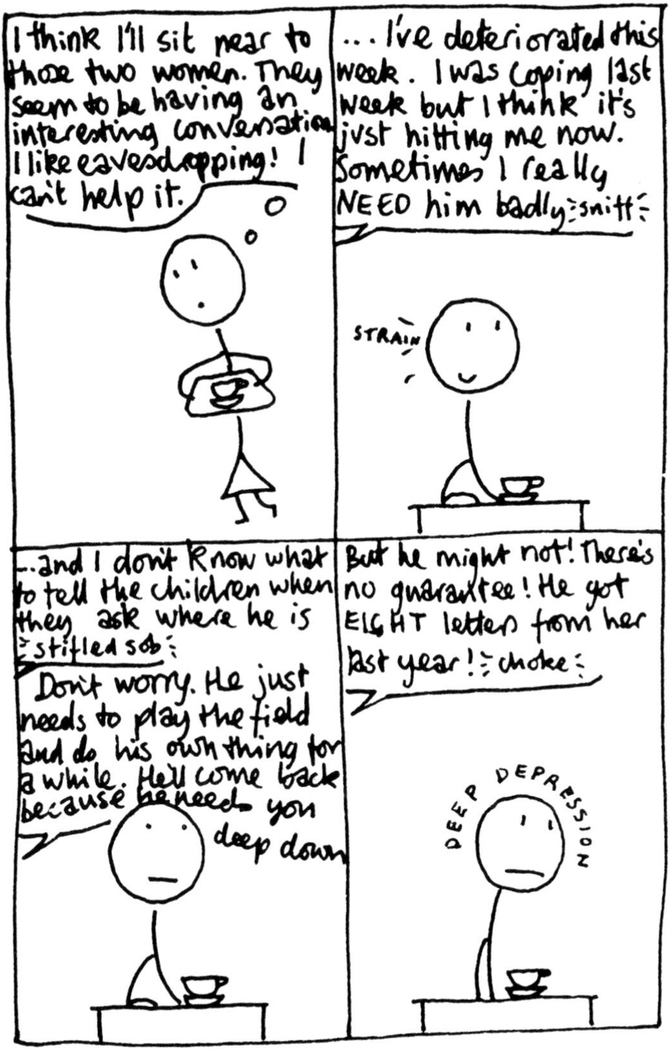
I think I'll sit near to those two women. They seem to be having an interesting conversation. I like eavesdropping! I can't help it.
... I've deteriorated this week. I was coping last week but I think it's just hitting me now. Sometimes I really NEED him badly :sniff:
STRAIN
...and I don't know what to tell the children when they ask where he is :stifled sob:
Don't worry. He just needs to play the field and do his own thing for a while. He'll come back because he needs you deep down
But he might not! There's no guarantee! He got EIGHT letters from her last year! :choke:
DEEP DEPRESSION

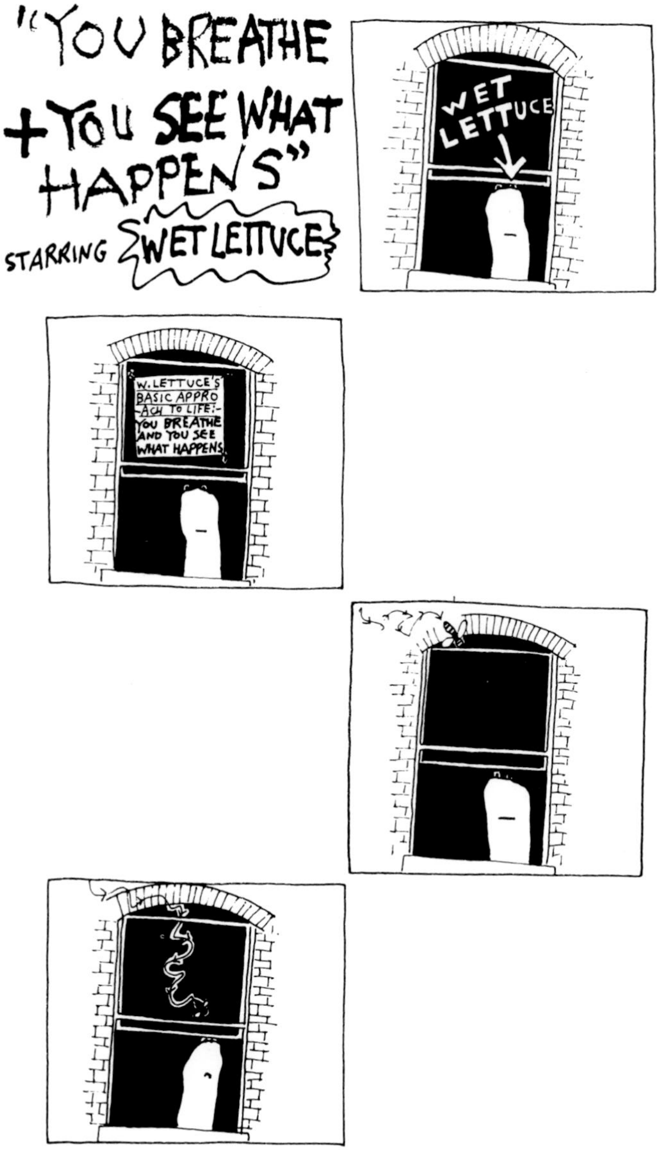
"YOU BREATHE + YOU SEE WHAT HAPPENS"
STARRING WET LETTUCE
WET LETTUCE
W. LETTUCE'S BASIC APPRO-ACH TO LIFE:- YOU BREATHE AND YOU SEE WHAT HAPPENS

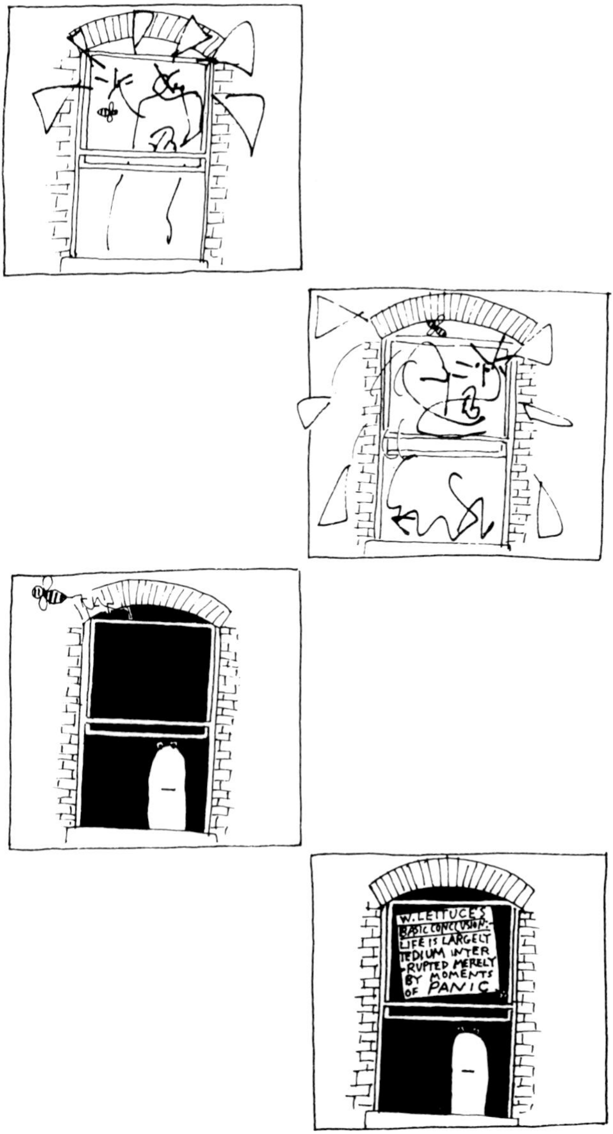
W. LETTUCE'S
BASIC CONCLUSION:-
LIFE IS LARGELY TEDIUM INTER-RUPTED MERELY BY MOMENTS OF PANIC.

Phallocracy fails the Female!

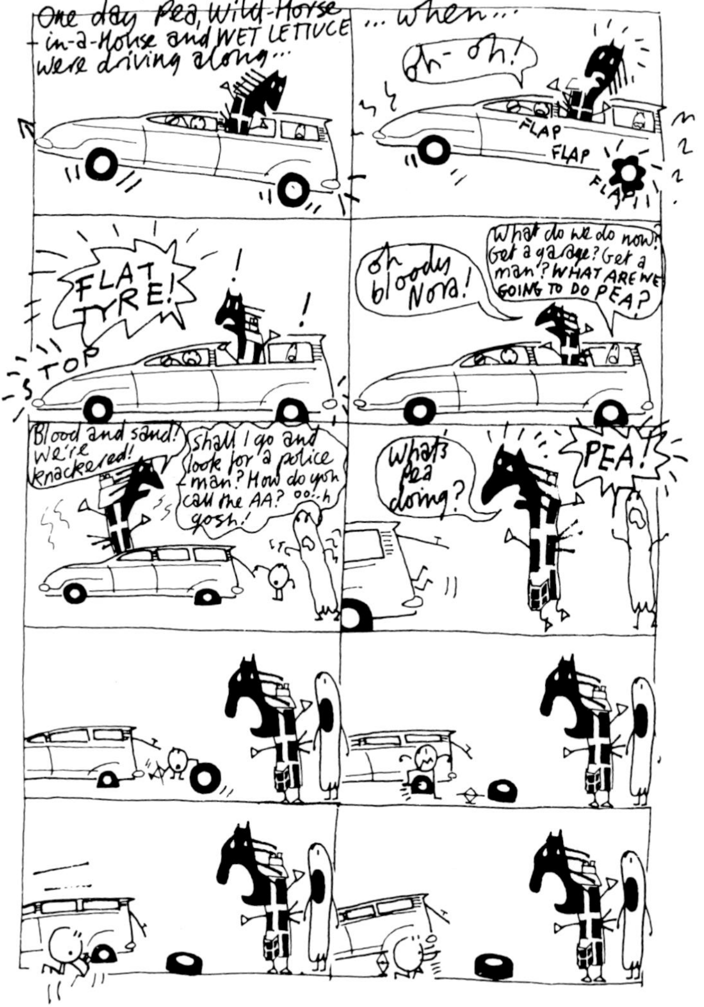
One day Pea, Wild-Horse-in-a-Horse and WET LETTUCE were driving along...
...when...
oh-oh!
FLAP
FLAP
FLAP
FLAT TYRE!
STOP
oh bloody Nora!
What do we do now? Get a garage? Get a man? WHAT ARE WE GOING TO DO PEA?
Blood and sand! We're knackered!
Shall I go and look for a police man? How do you call the AA? oo..h gosh!
What's Pea doing?
PEA!

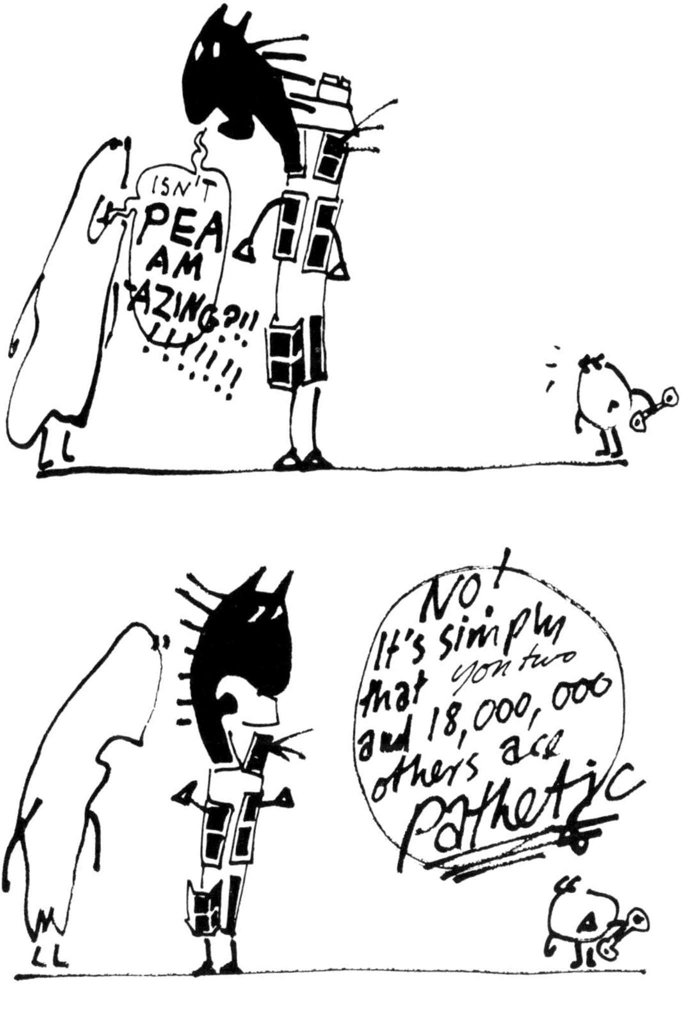
ISN'T PEA AM AZING?!! !!!!!!!!!
No! It's simply that you two and 18,000,000 others are PATHETIC

Wet Lettuce Luck

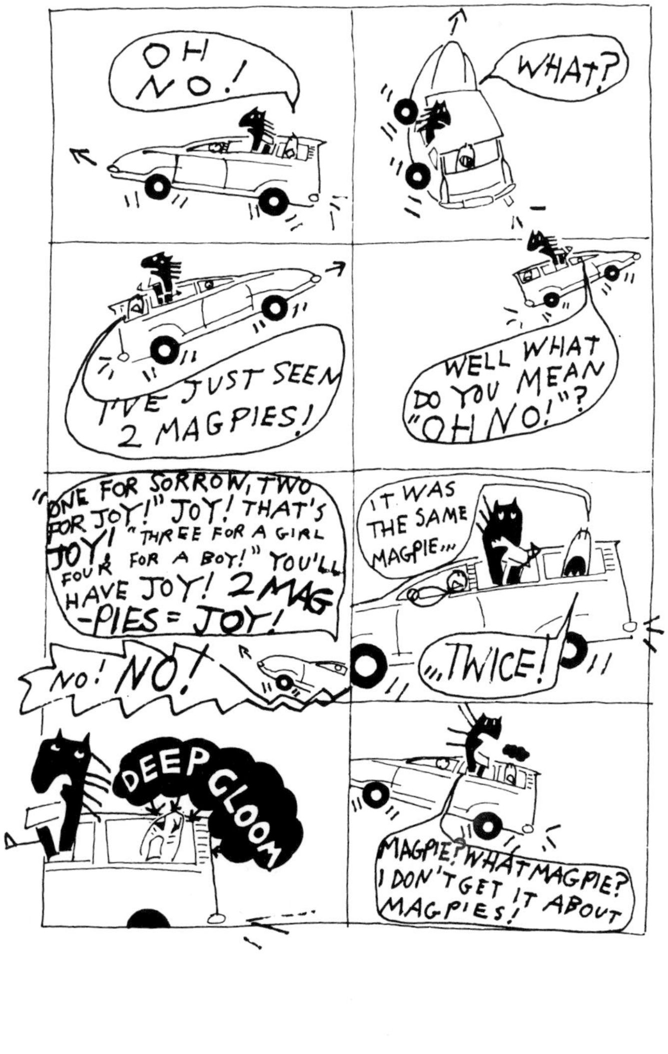
OH NO!
WHAT?
I'VE JUST SEEN 2 MAGPIES!
WELL WHAT DO YOU MEAN "OH NO!"?
"ONE FOR SORROW, TWO FOR JOY!" JOY! THAT'S JOY! "THREE FOR A GIRL FOUR FOR A BOY!" YOU'LL HAVE JOY! 2 MAG-PIES = JOY!
IT WAS THE SAME MAGPIE...
NO! NO!
...TWICE!
DEEP GLOOM
MAGPIE? WHAT MAGPIE? I DON'T GET IT ABOUT MAGPIES!

WHY DID YOU HANG THAT LAMPSHADE SO LOW?
At home with PEA
TO PUNISH TALL PEOPLE

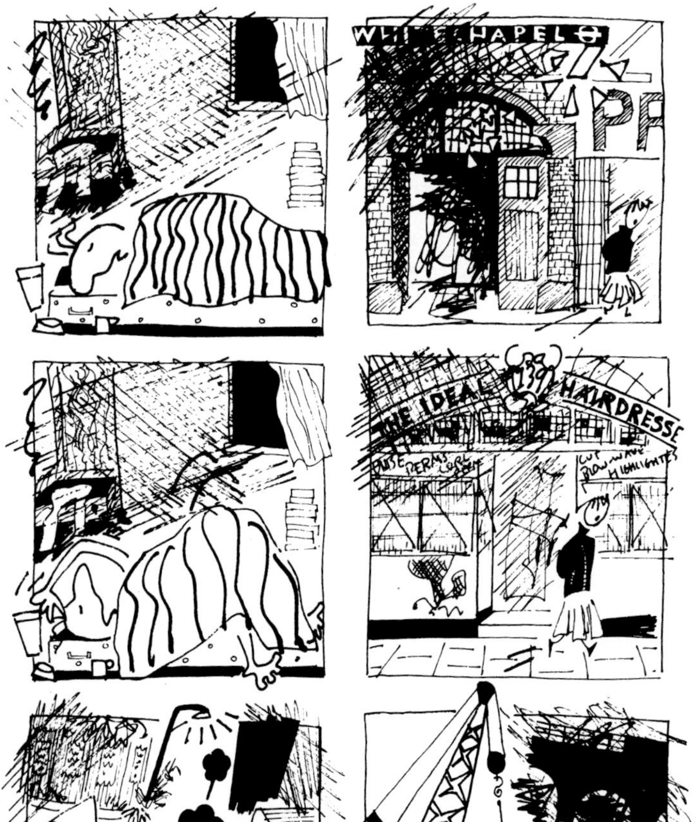
WHITECHAPEL
PR
THE IDEAL
HAIRDRESSE
PERMS
CUT
HIGHLIGHTS
SCREAM FOR CREAM!

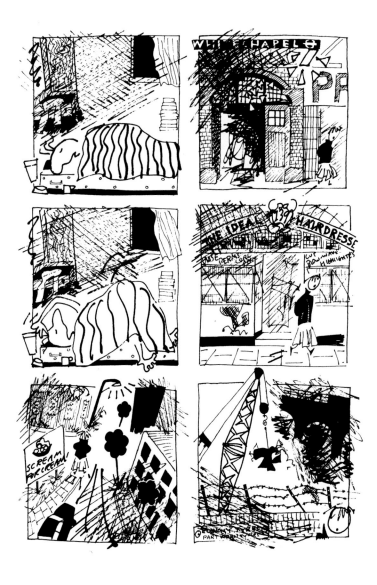

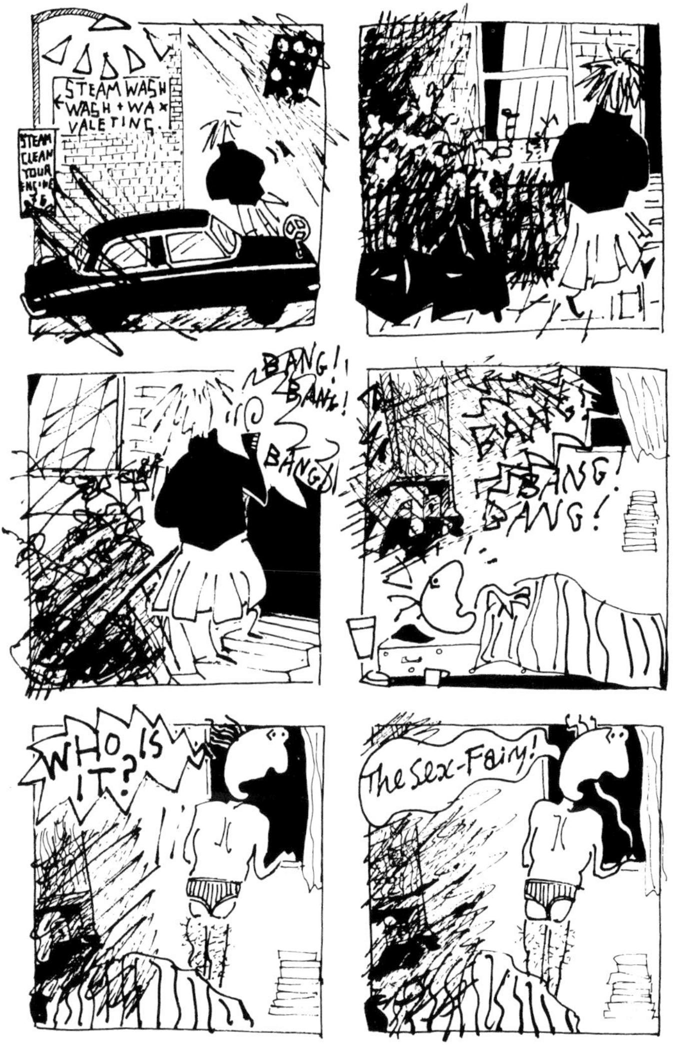
STEAM WASH
WASH + WAX
VALETING.
STEAM CLEAN YOUR ENGINE
BANG! BANG! BANG!
BANG! BANG!
WHO IS IT?
The Sex-Fairy!

CAN YOU TAKE ON PRE-FEMINIST MAN? The management of PRE-FEMINIST MAN requires a lot of skill! A novice should not rush in blindly, and even an EXPERIENCED HAND should be prepared for a LONG SLOG UPHILL! RADICAL RE-STRUCTURING OF MIND-SETS is the name of the game when dealing with PRE-FEMINIST MAN ... and a point to remember ... PRE-FEMINIST MAN has had many years to become well entrenched in his attitudes and setbacks WILL OCCUR ... however ... patience and tenacity are often rewarded ... A RE-CONDITIONED GENTLEMAN of age 40+ can knock the spots off a callow toyboy who's never read a book in his life anyday!

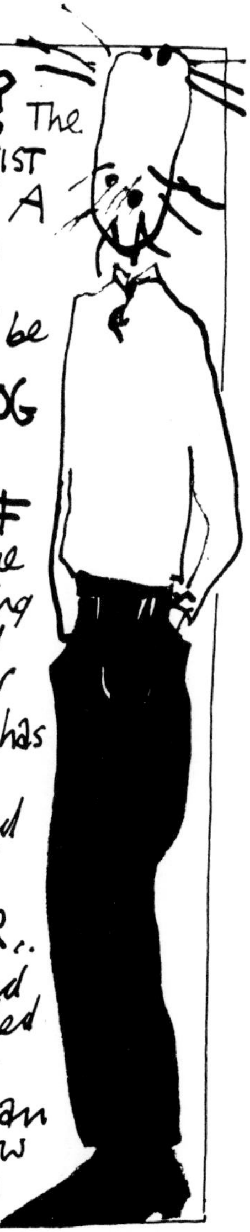

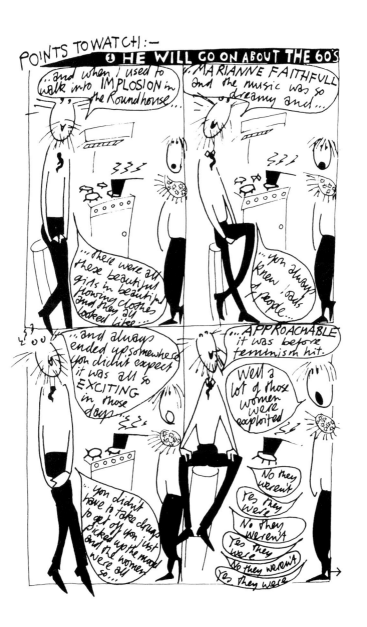

you know...
...what I can't help noticing...
...as I walk around town...
...which disgusts and appals me...
...and its ALL MEN'S fault! Bloody men they ought to be LOCKED UP...
...then WOMEN could reclaim the streets! YAY!
YAY!
If you notice ONE you notice 10,000,000...
...GOBS OF SPIT on the pavement!

Irritating Foibles of John
LET'S GET OUT OF HERE! THEY'RE GOING TO RIP US OFF!
Menu
...Tightness...

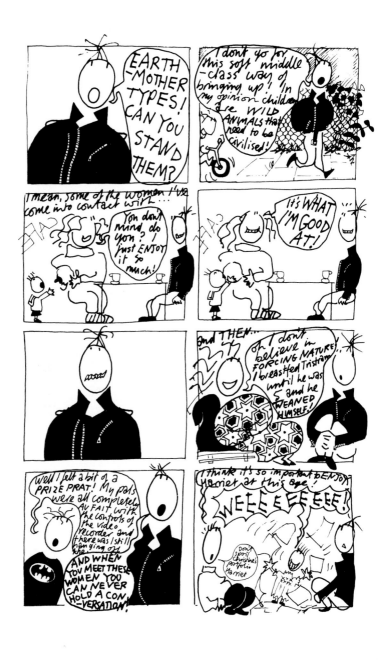

OLD HIPPY PLATITUDES

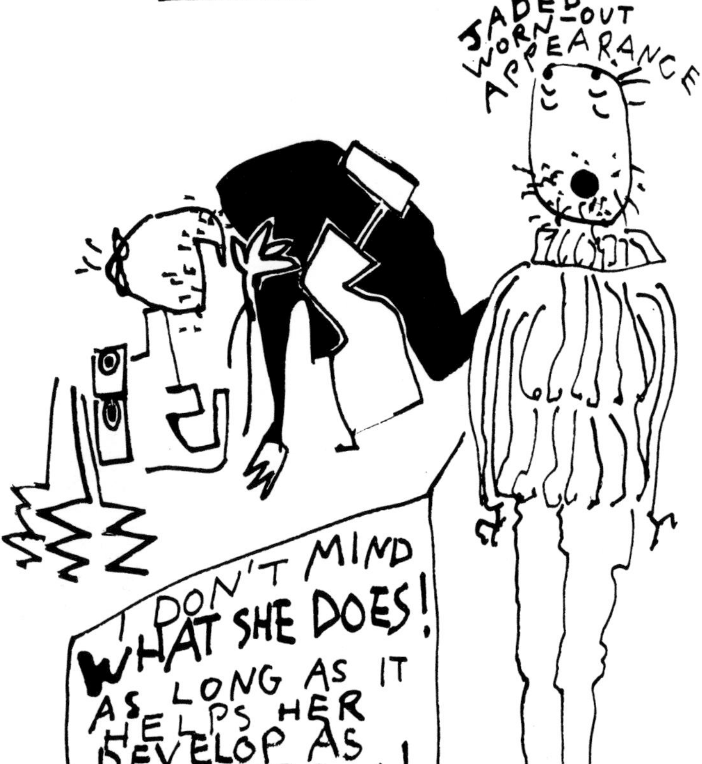
JADED WORN-OUT APPEARANCE
I DON'T MIND WHAT SHE DOES! AS LONG AS IT HELPS HER DEVELOP AS A PERSON!

BITE THE DUST

NEW-AGE FEMINIST GREENMEN ?
Are you AWARE when you ovulate? I think it's so IMPORTANT for a woman to be IN TUNE with her body!
click!
...GIVE ADVICE!

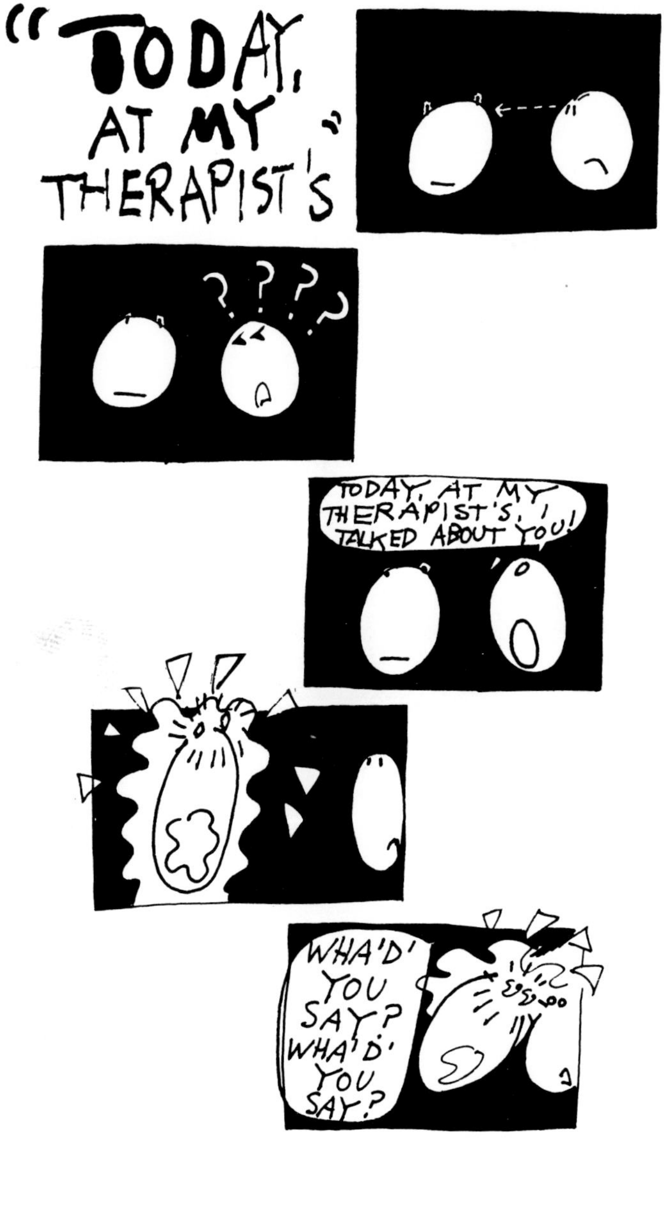
"TODAY, AT MY THERAPIST'S"
TODAY, AT MY THERAPIST'S, I TALKED ABOUT YOU!
WHA'D' YOU SAY? WHA'D' YOU SAY?

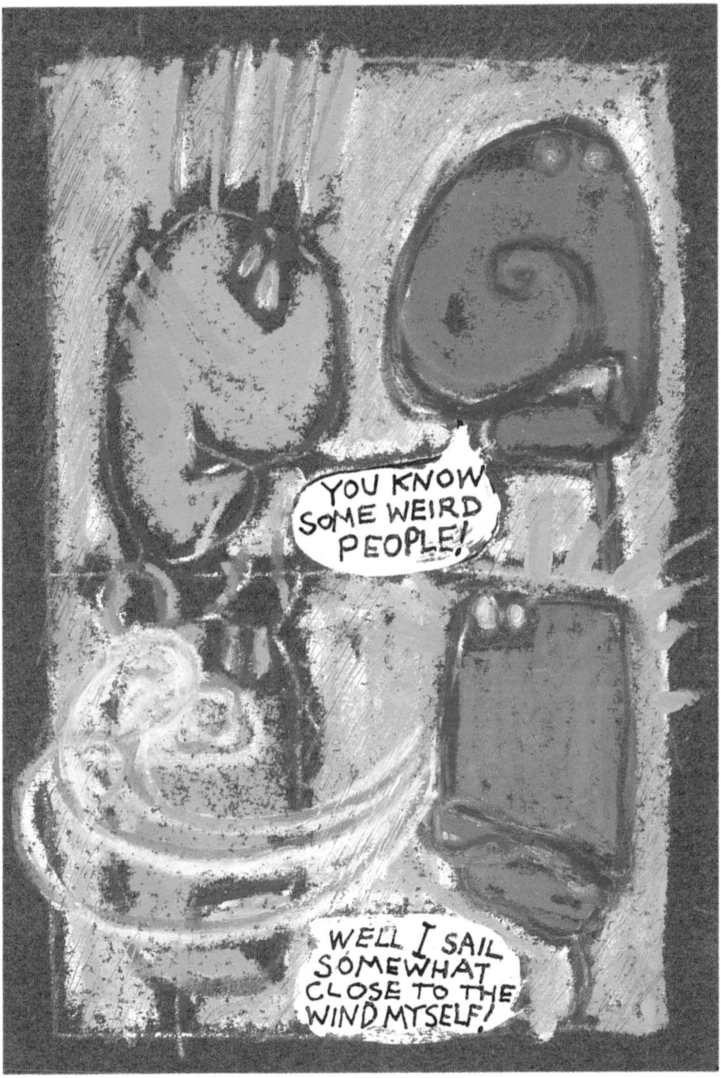
YOU KNOW SOME WEIRD PEOPLE!
WELL I SAIL SOMEWHAT CLOSE TO THE WIND MYSELF!

PEA... you know how recently... with all this therapy I've been doing ... groups + stuff...
... how I've been WORKING ON MYSELF and LOOKING AT MYSELF in order to isolate the causes in the past...
which have gone towards creating my particular reality in the present ... and how I'm into generally DEALING WITH MY STUFF...
... + CLEARING MY BLOCKS + how in the here + now I really am committed to FUNDAMENTALLY CHANGING MY PATTERNS with the ultimate goal of...
... hopefully leading a MORE FULLY REALISED EXISTANCE ON THIS PLANET...
yes
Well, there's something in this that I feel is holding me back
oh yes. what?
um... Being called "Wet lettuce"
IT'S THE FIRST STEP ON A PATH TO A NEW WAY OF BEING! It's a tentative step but a hopeful step! It's a statement of comm-itment...

...a confirmation of faith in an alternative possibility ... that fate CAN twist, that truth CAN break...
...that tables CAN turn and boots change feet!
... that visualisation CAN realise + MY DESIRES MANI-FEST!
...say "PO"!
In the beginning you must have the thought! The thought is the seed! Dare to think!
Dare to cast your seed/thoughts onto the fertile ground of the totally unlimited future!
You see Pea, WE CREATE the future!
Casting abroad our seed/thoughts ... nourishing them with POSITIVE ACTION...
WEEDS
... perpetually visualising THE BEST... WEEDING OUT all choking, life-sapping NEGATIVITY!
WE ARE THE GARDENERS OF OUR LIVES! WE HAVE THE POWER + WE CAN DO IT! I CAN do it... and this ... what I'm telling you this first step is...

I'M CHANGING MY NAME!
WHAT?!!!
What to?
Lettuce
I'm dropping the wet.
WHAT?
I can't get used to that! I'll never get used to that! As far as I'm concerned you're "WET LETTUCE"
You always HAVE BEEN "Wet Lettuce" and you always WILL BE Wet Lettuce! To call you by any other name would seem wrong! I couldn't get used to it!
No way.
Well... I'm asking you .. as a FRIEND
.. to try.
If you truly care about me ... and are committed .. as I am .. to my development. It wouldn't be difficult. I'm just dropping ½ of the name I used to be called!
Oh ... I see ... so what is it you're dropping... "LETTUCE" is it?... OK ... "WET"!
I'll call you WET hmm... WET that's short and unforgettable! WET!!!
LETTUCE!!!

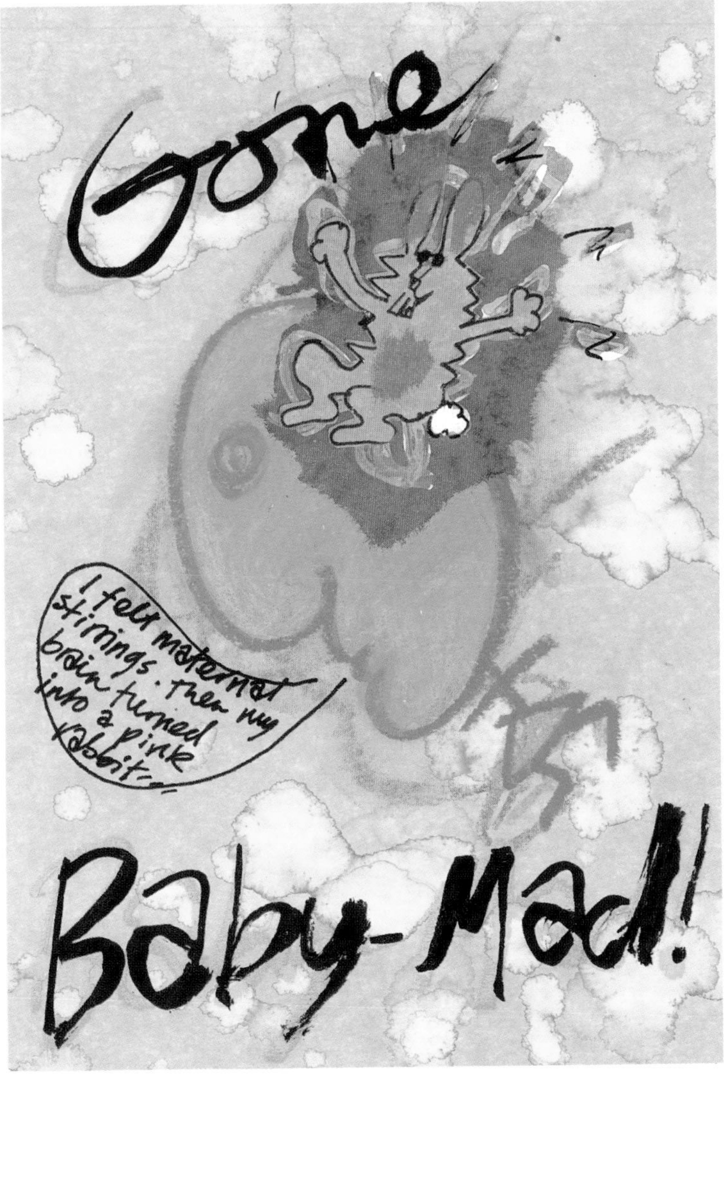
Gone
I felt maternal stirrings. Then my brain turned into a pink rabbit...
Baby-Mad!

You can GO OFF sex can't you?
UNBEARABLE
LIGHTNESS OF BEING
UNBEARABLE
DARKNESS OF BEING
WHAT DO YOU MEAN?
?
oh... I don't know... I just think I'd rather be force-fed 8 gallons of custard

I TALK TO PEOPLE
TORTURING MYSELF MENTALLY
WHAT HAVE YOU BEEN DOING?

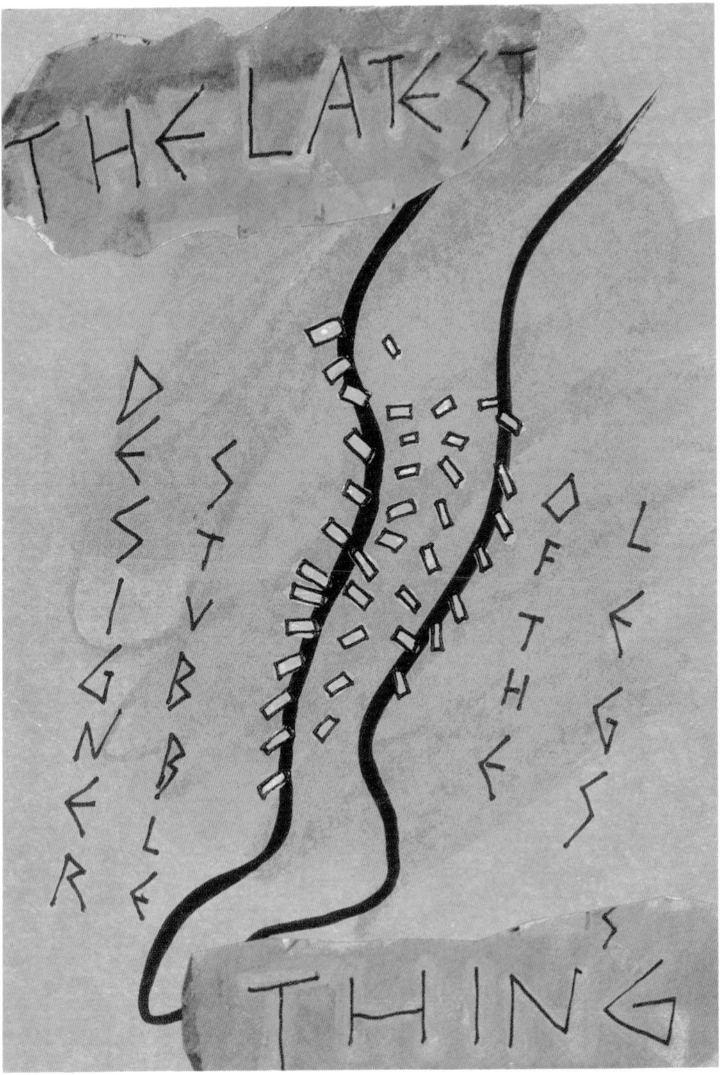
THE LATEST
DESIGNER
STVBBLE
OF THE
LEGS
THING